Steve Jobs

by Joanne Mattern

Content Consultant

Nanci R. Vargus, Ed.D.
Professor Emeritus, University of Indianapolis

Reading Consultant

Jeanne Clidas, Ph.D.

Children's Press®
An Imprint of Scholastic Inc.
New York Toronto London Auckland Sydney
Mexico City New Delhi Hong Kong
Danbury, Connecticut

Cataloging-in-Publication Data is available from the Library of Congress

ISBN 978-0-531-24739-6 (lib. bdg.)
ISBN 978-0-531-24705-1 (pbk.)

Produced by Spooky Cheetah Press
Poem by Jodie Shepherd

© 2013 by Scholastic Inc.

All rights reserved. Published in 2013 by Children's Press, an imprint of Scholastic Inc.

Printed in China 62

SCHOLASTIC, CHILDREN'S PRESS, ROOKIE BIOGRAPHIES®, and associated logos are trademarks and/or registered trademarks of Scholastic Inc.

1 2 3 4 5 6 7 8 9 10 R 22 21 20 19 18 17 16 15 14 13

Photographs © 2013: Alamy Images: 31 top (Aurora Photos), 20 (Gallo Images), 16, 31 center top (Moviestore Collection Ltd.); AP Images: 24 (Diane Bondareff), 31 bottom (Disney, Garth Vaughan), cover (Jeff Chiu), 11 (Sipa); Corbis Images: 27 (Alan Greth/ZUMA Press), 12 (Paul Sakuma/AP); Getty Images: 15, 30 left (Alexandra Wyman), 19 (John G. Mabanglo/AFP), 28 (Kevork Djansezian), 4 (Tony Avelar/Bloomberg); iStockphoto/craftvision: 3 top left, 31 center bottom; Photo Researchers/Peter Menzel: 8; Superstock, Inc.: 3 top right, 3 bottom, 30 right (Oleksiy Maksymenko/All Canada Photos), 23 (Phanie).

Maps by XNR Productions, Inc.

Table of Contents

Meet Steve Jobs

Thanks to Steve Jobs, we have the iPad, the iPhone, and iTunes. Steve was an innovator (in-uh-VAY-tor). That means he came up with a lot of new ideas. Many of Steve's ideas changed the way people live and work every day.

Steve shows off the new iPad in 2010.

Steven Paul Jobs was born on February 24, 1955, in San Francisco, California. He was **adopted** by Paul and Clara Jobs soon after he was born.

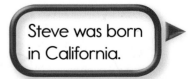

Steve was born in California.

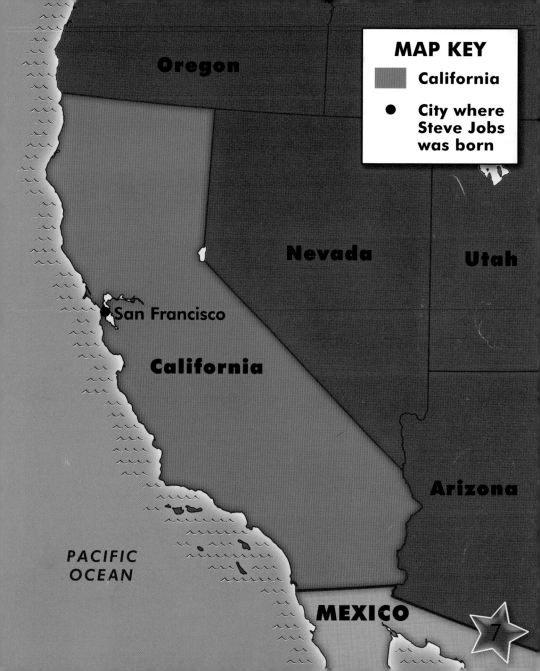

MAP KEY

California

● City where
Steve Jobs
was born

Oregon

Nevada

Utah

San Francisco

California

Arizona

PACIFIC
OCEAN

MEXICO

7

This is Steve's garage, where he worked with his dad. This is also where he built his first computer.

Steve's father liked to build things. He taught his son how to build things, too. Paul and Steve shared a workbench in the garage. They worked on many projects together.

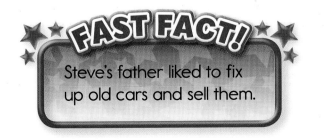

FAST FACT!

Steve's father liked to fix up old cars and sell them.

9

Computer Wizards

Steve Jobs and his friend Steve Wozniak also liked to build things in Jobs's garage. They started a company called Apple. They built a computer called the Apple II. It was the first computer to have a color screen.

Wozniak

Jobs

Jobs and Steve "Woz" Wozniak in 1976.

One day, Steve visited another computer company. He saw people using a mouse to point and click on the screen. Steve thought this was a great idea. He made the mouse a big part of Apple's next computer.

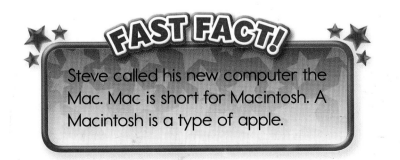

FAST FACT!

Steve called his new computer the Mac. Mac is short for Macintosh. A Macintosh is a type of apple.

What's NeXT?

In 1985, Steve left Apple. He started a new computer company called NeXT. When he was visiting a school to talk about NeXT computers, Steve met Laurene Powell. The two married in 1991. They later had three children: Reed Paul, Erin Sienna, and Eve.

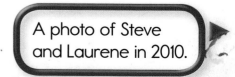

A photo of Steve and Laurene in 2010.

14

15

Around the same time, Steve bought a computer **animation** company. He renamed the **studio** Pixar. In 1995, Pixar made the world's first-ever computer-animated movie. It was called *Toy Story*. The movie was a huge hit!

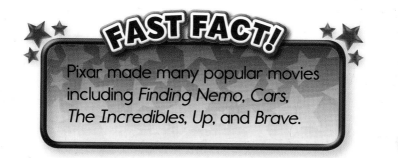

FAST FACT!

Pixar made many popular movies including *Finding Nemo, Cars, The Incredibles, Up,* and *Brave.*

17

An Apple a Day

Meanwhile, Steve's old company was not doing well. People at Apple asked him to come back. He did. And in 1998, Steve helped develop a new computer. It was called the iMac.

The iMac was available in different colors.

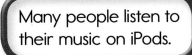

Many people listen to their music on iPods.

Steve saw that people liked listening to music on the Internet. So he created **software** that helped people buy and store music. He called it iTunes. Later Apple made a small music player called the iPod.

FAST FACT!

The iPod was a huge hit. By 2011, about 300 million iPods had been sold all over the world.

Then Steve worked on creating a cell phone that would be better than any other. The result was the iPhone. People could use an iPhone to do so much more than make phone calls!

People can use the iPhone to surf the Internet, send e-mails, play games, and more.

23

In 2010, Steve introduced a tablet computer called the iPad. A tablet is a small computer that you can hold in your hands. People could buy books and read them right on the iPad screen. They could also listen to music, play games, and do many other things.

Thousands of people waited in line at Apple stores to buy the new iPad.

25

Steve's Final Days

In the summer of 2011, Steve left his job at Apple. He had been sick with cancer since 2003. On October 5, 2011, Steve passed away.

Apple headquarters in Cupertino, California.

Timeline of Steve Jobs's Life

1984
introduces
Macintosh computer

1955
born on
February 24

1976
forms Apple Computers
with Steve Wozniak

> People left notes at Apple stores and sent text messages and e-mails to the company. They said how sorry they were that Steve was gone.

People all over the world felt sad when Steve Jobs died. Millions of people use Apple products every day. Many believe that Steve's amazing ideas changed the world.

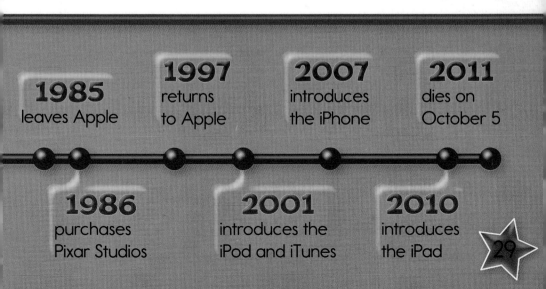

1985
leaves Apple

1997
returns
to Apple

2007
introduces
the iPhone

2011
dies on
October 5

1986
purchases
Pixar Studios

2001
introduces the
iPod and iTunes

2010
introduces
the iPad

A Poem About Steve Jobs

We owe so much to that little "i."

Imagine the world without it; just try!

iTunes, iPhones, iPads—too many to mention—

each was amazing Steve Jobs's invention.

You Can Be an Innovator

- You can think of new things to make or new ways to do things.

- Believe in yourself! Keep on doing what feels right to you—even if people tell you your idea might not work.

Glossary

adopt (uh-DOPT): take a child into a family and become his or her legal parents

animation (an-uh-MAY-shun): cartoon drawings shown very quickly one after another on a screen so that it appears as if the drawings are moving

software (SAFT-wair): programs used by a computer

studio (STOO-dee-oh): a place where movies are made or where artists work

Index

Facts for Now

Visit this Scholastic Web site for more information on Steve Jobs:
www.factsfornow.scholastic.com
Enter the keywords **Steve Jobs**

About the Author

Joanne Mattern has written more than 250 books for children. She especially likes writing biographies because she loves to learn about real people and the things they do. Joanne also enjoys writing about science, nature, and history. She grew up in New York State and still lives there with her husband, her four children, and an assortment of pets.